Common Birds of The Brinton Museum and Bighorn Mountains Foothills

Jacqueline L. Canterbury & Paul A. Johnsgard

Sponsored by Bighorn Audubon, Sheridan, Wyoming

Zea Books

Lincoln, Nebraska 2017

Osprey

ISBN: 978-1-60962-114-8
doi:10.13014/K2SQ8XK8

Composed in Segoe UI types.

Zea Books are published by the University of Nebraska–Lincoln Libraries
Electronic (pdf) edition available online at http://digitalcommons.unl.edu/zeabook/
Print edition available from http://www.lulu.com/spotlight/unlib

Contents

Introduction and Acknowledgments

The primary reason this book was written is to give birders and naturalists an opportunity to more easily identify and learn about the birds that might be readily seen at The Brinton Museum near Big Horn, Wyoming. We selected the most abundant, typical, and interesting birds from the 114 species that have been regularly reported from The Brinton, especially those species occurring year-round or as breeders during the summer months. These species also include some of the most typical birds of the high plains and mountain habitats of the Bighorn Mountains region.

One of the objectives of this book is to help teach the "average" person how to identify birds. To that end, it provides information on when and where to find them. We also provide brief information on each species' identification, voice, status, and habitats as primary learning tools. "Identification" describes the important visual characteristics (field marks) of a bird, "voice" provides information on its songs and calls, "status" indicates its relative regional and seasonal abundance, and "habitats and ecology" provides a brief description of those habitats and environmental features that the species prefers.

The species list was generated from the monthly birding events hosted by The Brinton that began in 2011 and the *Bird Checklist for The Brinton Museum* (Canterbury *et al.*, 2016). Much of this information, including the notes on regional birding, was derived from an earlier book, *Birds and Birding in Wyoming's Bighorn Mountains Region* (Canterbury *et al.*, 2013). The species descriptions were primarily derived from Paul Johnsgard's *Birds of the Rocky Mountains* (1986) with additions and taxonomic updates from the Birds of North America online (Cornell Lab of Ornithology) and the "Checklist" of the (recently reorganized) American Ornithological Society. The seasonal occurrence for each species was derived from eBird data, years 2000 through 2016, and Faulkner's *Birds of Wyoming* (2010), together with notes from local birders. We also acknowledge Dr. Craig Benkman and Dr. Scott Johnson for their contributions to the species accounts.

We especially wish to acknowledge Kenneth L. Schuster, director and chief curator, and Barbara McNab, curator of exhibitions and museum education, for The Brinton Museum as well as the Bighorn Audubon chapter of National Audubon Society for cosponsoring the monthly birding events at The Brinton. This event has given us the opportunity to appreciate and understand the birds that inhabit The Brinton Museum and its surrounding Bighorn foothills and to record valuable observations. We are also grateful to Paul Royster and Linnea Fredrickson at the University of Nebraska–Lincoln Libraries for taking on this project and producing such a fine result.

Financial help in defraying publishing costs was gratefully received from members of the Bighorn Audubon chapter of the National Audubon Society, including a generous donation from Claudia Colnar on behalf of her mother, Lana Colnar, to whom this book is dedicated. Photographs are by the authors, Dr. Jackie Canterbury, Dr. Paul Johnsgard, and Dave Rinaldo of Scorched Earth Photos. Hand drawings are by Paul Johnsgard.

Part I. The Brinton Museum and Its Birds

Introduction and History of the Quarter Circle A Ranch

Kenneth L. Schuster, Director and Chief Curator, The Brinton Museum

The property on which The Brinton Museum is located was homesteaded by the Clark family in 1880. They first lived in a dugout and then, like most settlers, built a wooden house on top of the dugout. Within a decade, they had sold the property to the Becker family, who then sold the property to William Moncreiffe. The Moncreiffes established the Quarter Circle A Ranch and built the Ranch House in 1892. Of Scottish descent, William and his brother, Malcolm Moncreiffe, sold some twenty thousand horses to the British cavalry during the Boer War.

In 1923 the Moncreiffes sold the 640-acre Quarter Circle A Ranch headquarters to Bradford Brinton. Mr. Brinton was born in Illinois in 1880 and graduated from the Sheffield School of Engineering at Yale University in 1904. He went to work for the family company, Grand Detour Plow Company, which was later acquired by the J. I. Case Threshing Machine Company, from which he retired in 1926.

Brinton used the Ranch House at the Quarter Circle A as a vacation home, spending several months each year in Big Horn. He also kept an apartment in New York City and maintained a home in Santa Barbara, California.

Extensive renovations were made to the Ranch House during 1927 and 1928. The upstairs was remodeled; a wing was added on the west end to house a master bedroom, bath, and dressing room; and the existing wraparound porch was removed and the sun porches and bay windows added. During the same period, the Little Goose Creek Lodge and the horse barn were also built. An avid collector of fine art, Native American artifacts, firearms, and books, Brinton filled his home with fine and beautiful items. He was personal friends with many artists, such as Ed Borein, Hans Kleiber, and Bill Gollings, whose art decorated the Ranch House. He also collected works by Frederic Remington, C. M. Russell, and John J. Audubon.

Brinton was married for ten years. However, the marriage ended in divorce, and his wife moved to Santa Barbara, California, with their twin daughters, Patricia and Barbara, who had been born in 1926. The girls visited their father during several summers at the Quarter Circle A Ranch. In 1936 Brinton died from complications following surgery. His will left the Quarter Circle A Ranch property to his sister, Helen Brinton.

Helen Brinton summered on the ranch in Big Horn and spent winters at her ranch near Phoenix, Arizona. She died in 1960. In her will, Helen Brinton specified that the Quarter Circle A Ranch be kept as a memorial to her brother, Bradford, and she established a trust for that purpose. Helen wished that the public should enjoy Bradford's magnificent collection of art and that the ranch land be kept in a natural state to provide sanctuary for birds and other wildlife.

The original gallery building was constructed in 1966 to better display The Brinton art collection. In 2015 the Forrest E. Mars, Jr. Building opened, which provided increased exhibit space and a modern storage facility. In addition to The Brinton collection, the Forrest E.

Mars, Jr. Building also houses the Gallatin Collection of Plains Indian Art and Artifacts and numerous pieces of fine art, photographs, and sculpture.

Bradford and Helen Brinton left an enduring legacy of a golden era in this early twentieth-century gentleman's working ranch. The Wild West had been tamed, the vast rangelands fenced, and motorized vehicles were replacing horses. Americans were clinging to the images of hardy cowboys, noble Indians, and untamed land filled with birds and wild beasts. Bradford and Helen Brinton have helped preserve the feeling of the West at that time for all of us to enjoy today.

Sharp-tailed Grouse

The Natural Environment and Habitats of the Brinton

The Brinton Museum lies along the foothills of the Bighorn Mountains. This relatively isolated mountain range of north-central Wyoming reaches a maximum of 13,167 feet and covers about one million acres. The plant communities of the Bighorns are similar to those in other parts of the Rocky Mountains. The Brinton lies on the eastern slope of the mountains, where the drier lower-elevation grasslands grade both to foothills and into higher-elevation forests and finally terminate in the cold-adapted alpine vegetation (Meyer *et al.*, 2005).

The major plant communities of the Bighorn Mountains have been shaped by many factors, including temperature, precipitation, soils, and elevation (Faulkner, 2010; Knight *et al.*, 2014). The transition from the dry, low-elevation grassland to the moist, high-elevation forest can be seen from the grounds of The Brinton. This rather predictable plant transition also occurs with birds: the more arid grassland supports species such as the Western Meadowlark and Vesper Sparrow, while the higher-elevation foothills and forests support the Mountain Bluebird, Red Crossbill, and White-breasted and Red-breasted Nuthatches. The riparian community exists where Little Goose Creek flows through the property. The importance of this habitat type cannot be overstated. It has been estimated that 75 percent of the local animals depend on the riparian community at some time in their life cycle (Knight *et al.*, 2014). Additionally, The Brinton gardens and grounds provide an urban landscape that features notable bird species such as the House Wren, American Robin, and Calliope Hummingbird. A description of the area's major plant communities and associated birds of The Brinton follow:

Grasslands: The central Great Plains grasslands extend westward into Wyoming, where the forested eastern flank of the Bighorn Mountains transitions to the mixed-grass prairies of the plains. Grasses such as Canada wild rye, June grass, and needle-and-thread are found at these lower elevations (Knight *et al.*, 2014). The native grassland community supports such prairie species as the Lark Bunting, Lark Sparrow, Horned Lark, Western Meadowlark, Vesper Sparrow, and Sharp-tailed Grouse.

Mountain foothills: The mountain foothills provide a transition between the lower-elevation grassland and the forest community. Shrub thickets, often in draws along the foothills, are dominated by sagebrush, serviceberry, snowberry, sumac, and mountain mahogany (Faulkner, 2010). The evergreen curl-leaf mountain-mahogany is a dominant shrub on the Bighorn foothills (Knight *et al.*, 2014). Mountain Bluebirds and White-breasted and Red-breasted Nuthatches can be observed along the higher-elevation foothills and forests.

Riparian areas: After dropping more than 4,000 feet and entering a steep canyon, Little Goose Creek flows out of the Bighorn Mountains and passes through The Brinton grounds. The plants along the river margins, referred to as the riparian zone, are dominated by old, large narrowleaf cottonwoods interspersed with aspen, ponderosa pine, boxelder, and green ash. Understory shrubs, which provide important cover for birds, include willow, hawthorn, and chokecherry. Bird species that can be found along the riparian corridor include the American Dipper, Yellow Warbler, Warbling and Red-eyed Vireos, Black-capped Chickadee, Great Blue Heron, Tree Swallow, Song Sparrow, and Sandhill Crane.

Wetlands and ponds: Sites where water is present most or all the time are especially important. Water provides many features critical to aquatic birds. Wetlands and ponds have vegetation such as emergent cattails, rushes, and sedges that often provide important nesting cover and food sources. Whether during migrations or the breeding season, the ponds are rich places to view a diversity of species such as Red-winged Blackbirds and the occasional Marsh Wren. Yellow and Yellow-rumped Warblers frequent the tall willows that surround the ponds. Ducks and geese breed along their shorelines, and many birds—such as the Killdeer, Spotted Sandpiper, and various swallows, including the abundant Cliff Swallow that nests nearby—find abundant insect food below, on, and above the water surface.

Urban landscape: The Brinton has developed a small urban garden with an emphasis on pollinator plants for birds, bees, and butterflies. Calliope Hummingbirds can be observed in summer hovering over penstemons, gilias, and salvias, and Rufous Hummingbirds are regular July visitors. The Brinton also supports a magnificent diversity of native and non-native trees, including ponderosa pine, plains cottonwood, Scots pine, silver maple, blue spruce, linden, and red maple. Many of these trees were planted in the early to mid-1900s and now represent old-growth trees.

Old-growth trees are very important for cavity-nesting birds. Some 85 species of North American birds excavate nesting holes, use natural cavities resulting from tree decay, or occupy holes created by other birds (Scott *et al.*, 1977). In fact, old trees are a critical factor for many birds that require them for their nesting. Primary excavators include the Downy Woodpecker, Red-naped Sapsucker, Northern Flicker, Black-capped Chickadee, Mountain Chickadee, White-breasted Nuthatch, and Red-breasted Nuthatch. Other local cavity- or crevice-nesting birds that may use such pre-excavated or natural cavities for nesting include the Wood Duck, Common Merganser, Turkey Vulture, Eastern Screech-Owl, American Kestrel, Tree Swallow, Brown Creeper, House Wren, Mountain Bluebird, European Starling, and House Sparrow.

Bighorn Audubon and The Brinton as an Important Bird Area

The Bighorn Audubon chapter of the National Audubon Society began the program "Birding at The Brinton" in 2011. Because of the popular Saturday events, countless people were provided the opportunity to view and document the birds on the grounds of The Brinton. A local bird checklist (Canterbury *et al.*, 2016) is available at The Brinton Museum store.

In November 2016, Bighorn Audubon, in cooperation with Audubon Rockies, and The Brinton Museum formed a partnership to designate 620 acres of The Brinton as an Important Bird Area (IBA). IBAs are part of a global conservation strategy that focuses attention on habitats and key bird species. IBAs provide essential habitat for one or more species of breeding, wintering, or migrating birds. This IBA designation recognizes the importance of The Brinton for birds nationally.

Status: Relative Bird Abundance and Seasonal Occurrence Terminology

The following terms are used in this book to describe relative bird abundance:

Abundant – Occurs at high density at appropriate seasons
Common – Expected in high numbers at appropriate seasons
Uncommon – Expected in low numbers at appropriate seasons

The following terms are used to describe seasonal occurrence:

Permanent resident – Present throughout the year establishing territories and breeding locally

Summer resident – Present in summer with local breeding proven or very likely

Winter migrant – A nonbreeding species that typically is present from fall to spring

Migrant – A nonbreeding species that passes through the area seasonally

Voice: Bird Songs and Calls

A song can be defined as a series of complex, often species-specific sounds produced for attracting a mate, announcing a breeding territory, or both. True "songbirds" of the species known as "higher" passerines ("oscines"), a scientific subgroup of the overall group of perching birds (Order Passeriformes), have complex vocal structures (the syrinx and associated muscles) and usually begin learning their song in the nest from parents and nearby neighbors. Young birds then practice those songs (as "sub-songs" or "rehearsed songs") until they are perfected ("crystalized"). As in humans, regional dialects often develop, particularly when birds are geographically isolated, such as in the Bighorn Mountains. Of the world's ten thousand bird species, about half of them technically "sing." Songbirds vocalize using learned or partially learned utterances; even birds like crows and ravens "sing" by this definition. There are also some intermediate groups (the non-oscine passerines), such as kingbirds, that inherit rather than learn their complex songs. Among most birds only males sing, although in some groups (such as phalaropes) the sexual functions are reversed and females establish territories and sing. Song diversity has the advantage of potentially allowing recognition of species, sexes, and individuals, such as pair or family members.

In contrast, "calls" are simpler vocalizations that are typically inherited and do not require a learning phase. Because of this, calls are both instinctively produced and understood by all the birds of a particular species. Calls are used for simple but important messages, such as alarm, pair and family contact, takeoff and landing, and more.

Birding Ethics and Recommendations

Birds play an important role in all of our natural ecosystems. It is important that we preserve them and their habitats by supporting conservation efforts and by maintaining and protecting both terrestrial and wetland habitats on our properties, including both planted trees and native woodlands. We should also avoid the use of pesticides on our lawns and gardens, keep cats from harming birds, and limit disturbance, especially during the breeding season. At The Brinton, please stay on the observed trails and avoid entering restricted areas. Disturbing a protected bird's nesting and perch sites can result in unnecessary stress and is a federal offense. Birders should keep an appropriate distance from all birds they observe. The Migratory Bird Treaty Act of 1918 is a federal law that makes it unlawful "to pursue, hunt, take, capture, kill or sell migratory birds." The statute does not discriminate between live or dead birds and also grants full protection to any bird parts, including feathers, eggs, and nests, even on private property. Do not use recordings to attract birds, as it causes unnecessary stress. When photographing birds, use a telephoto lens and maintain a discreet distance.

Part II. Profiles of 48 Common Local and Regional Birds

The following list of birds closely follows the *Bird Checklist for The Brinton Museum* (Canterbury *et al.*, 2016) and includes data gained from the monthly birding events that began in 2011 and were jointly hosted by The Brinton Museum and the Bighorn chapter of the National Audubon Society. Many have spent countless hours since then at The Brinton, watching, recording data, and simply enjoying birds.

It is hard to imagine a more appealing place for watching birds than The Brinton. The mature planted trees, streamside flora and animal life, diverse gardens, native upland meadows, and scattered wetlands provide a setting that is both beautiful and highly diverse ecologically. At not many places in the region can a person regularly see the American Dipper feeding in a swiftly flowing stream, watch nesting Cooper's Hawks and Great Horned Owls, hear the stirring territorial calls of breeding Sandhill Cranes echoing over mountain meadows, observe tiny Calliope Hummingbirds dancing from flower to flower through the summer months, and view Bald Eagles roosting in tall cottonwoods on a cold winter's eve. And this says nothing of the glorious western and historic regional art collection that The Brinton Museum offers visitors after they become exhausted from watching birds.

For this book, we selected 48 of the most common and interesting birds from the nearly 114 species that have been regularly reported from the Brinton area (Canterbury *et al.*, 2016; unpublished manuscript). This book combines the observations from that checklist, plus some additional common species reported from the surrounding Bighorn foothills area, encompassed by Brinton Road,

Highway 335 from Beaver Creek Road south to Red Grade Road, and extending to the US Forest Service boundary.

The species accounts for each bird provide information on species identification followed by a brief guide for recognizing distinctive songs and calls. The status section provides information on the relative abundance and seasonal occurrence of a species. This is followed by a brief description of those habitats and environmental features that the species prefers. The calendar at the end of each species account shows the species' documented occurrences for every week of the year in the Brinton area and can be helpful as a predictive tool for judging the possibilities of a species' seasonal presence, both locally and regionally. The "X" refers to recorded occurrences by month and week for the Sheridan area based on 2000–2016 eBird data and Faulkner's guide (2010). It is important to note that many migrant species may occur outside the seasonal occurrence calendar. Additionally, species that are classified as permanent residents may partially migrate out of a region for part of the year, only to be replaced by same-species migrants from other regions.

Finally, climate change is rapidly altering the regional abundance and distribution of birds by changing seasonal arrival and departure schedules, affecting geographic distribution gradients of birds, and altering seasonal breeding periods. For example, in neighboring Nebraska, average spring arrival times of more than two hundred species that were calculated for the six-decade period between the 1930s and the 1980s, now arrive two to three weeks earlier, and fall departure times are typically three to four weeks later, or overwintering may even occur (Johnsgard, 1988a; 1988b; 2009; 2015b). Additionally, spring arrival dates in Sheridan, particularly in 2017, suggest that many species are arriving up to two weeks earlier than expected. This trend is likely to continue.

Please submit to Bighorn Audubon details of sightings of any species not on The Brinton Museum checklist. A photograph and written documentation would be appreciated. Email to:

bighornaudubon@gmail.com

Belted Kingfisher

Ring-necked Pheasant (*Phasianus colchicus*)

Identification: The familiar "ring-necked" male hardly needs description; females may be confused with sharp-tailed grouse if their long tails and more generally mottled brownish plumage are not noted. This chicken-like bird has a long, pointed tail and long legs, and tends to strut across open fields. Their powerful breast muscles permit bursts of power, allowing them to flush almost vertically into the air.

Voice: Males utter a distinctive crowing call, a double-noted *caw-cawk*, during late winter and spring that can be heard for more than a half-mile. Pheasant calls are highly diverse and number from an estimated 16 to 24 call types (Giudice and Ratti, 2001).

Status: A common permanent-resident, nonnative species, the Ring-necked Pheasant was introduced to the United States from China in the late 1880s and early 1900s.

Habitats and Ecology: Breeding occurs mainly in native grasslands, edges of woodlands and marshes, irrigated agricultural areas, and small patches with tall grass and weedy forbs.

JAN	FEB	MAR	APR	MAY	JUNE	JULY	AUG	SEPT	OCT	NOV	DEC
xxxx	xxxx	xxxx	xxxx	xxxx	xxxx	xxxx	xxxx	xxxx	xxxx	xxxx	xxxx

Sharp-tailed Grouse (*Tympanuchus phasianellus*)

Identification: This "prairie grouse" is found mostly on open grasslands. It is mostly buffy white below with a short, pointed tail. It is lighter in color than the sage grouse or any of the forest grouse, and its pointed, mostly white tail, is shorter than a pheasant's. Its nostrils and legs are feathered, and males expose violet-colored "air sacs" (an inflated esophagus) during display.

Voice: In spring males establish territories in small mating clusters (leks). Displaying males use cooing and "cork-popping" calls during lek displays, and they produce rattlesnake-like feather-scraping sounds while dancing from rapid lateral movements of their rectrices (Connelly *et al.*, 1998; Johnsgard, 2002).

Status: Uncommon permanent resident.

Habitats and Ecology: Sharp-tailed Grouse are associated with native grasslands and mountain foothills, shrublands, and mixed-grass prairie at lower elevations. On winter nights they may burrow in snowdrifts. Wyoming numbers are highest in the Sheridan area (Faulkner, 2010).

JAN	FEB	MAR	APR	MAY	JUNE	JULY	AUG	SEPT	OCT	NOV	DEC
xxxx	xxxx	xxxx	xxxx	xxxx	xxxx	xxxx	xxxx	xxxx	xxxx	xxxx	xxxx

Great Blue Heron (*Ardea herodias*)

Identification: The Great Blue Heron is the largest of the common herons of the area and is mostly bluish gray with a black crown-stripe; a long, narrow crest; and a long, yellow bill. It flies ponderously with its long legs trailing and the head held back on the shoulders. During the summer it may be seen perching atop nesting trees; otherwise, it is usually found standing in shallow water, searching for aquatic prey.

Voice: This heron is mostly silent except during the breeding season when it uses a *roh-roh-roh* call at the nest site and a croaking call when threatened by rival males or other intruders.

Status: A common permanent resident, it is regular in small numbers in winter.

Habitats and Ecology: This species occurs along the major riparian areas where there are fish and suitable trees. Large cottonwoods near water are a favored location for colonial nesting colonies, where stick nests are constructed near the crowns of trees. Herons can be seen at The Brinton on both Little Goose and Trabing Creeks, even in winter. A heronry (with 11 nests in 2017) can be viewed on Brundage Lane in Sheridan.

JAN	FEB	MAR	APR	MAY	JUNE	JULY	AUG	SEPT	OCT	NOV	DEC
x x	x x	xxxx	xxxx	xxxx	xxxx	xxxx	xxxx	xxxx	xxxx	x x	x x

Turkey Vulture (*Cathartes aura*)

Identification: Usually seen in flight, this species soars for long periods on wings that are slightly uptilted and two-toned, with black feathers in front and gray behind. Their primaries expose long finger-like tips while gliding or soaring The unfeathered head is reddish in adults and appears small relative to the size of the wings and entirely blackish body.

Voice: Vultures do not sing or call because they lack a syrinx, the vocal organ responsible for sound, yet vultures can produce a low hissing sound during flight.

Status: Common summer resident, it winters in the southern U.S. and Mexico.

Habitats and Ecology: The Turkey Vulture is a scavenger species that consumes the carcasses of mostly larger animals, such as livestock and deer, which it finds visually as well as by using its remarkable olfactory abilities. Vultures can often be seen soaring above on thermals, with few or no wingbeats. Nesting occurs in steep river valleys; the eggs are placed on bare cliff ledges, under rock overhangs, or in crevices. The nests can also be placed on or near the ground in hollow logs or in large snags, when available. The birds return to the same nest site year after year.

JAN	FEB	MAR	APR	MAY	JUNE	JULY	AUG	SEPT	OCT	NOV	DEC
			xxxx	xxxx	xxxx	xxxx	xxxx	xxxx	xxxx	x	

15

Osprey (*Pandion haliaetus*)

Identification: This raptor's white underparts, except for black "wrist marks" on the underside of the wings, are distinctive field marks, as are its long wings, which are usually held at a slightly bent angle, rather than horizontally as the eagles do. Ospreys are highly adapted for fish catching, which they snatch while in flight.

Voice: The male display call is a high-pitched slow *chirp*. The threat call, produced when a rival male appears, sounds like a high-pitched whistle.

Status: Uncommon summer resident. Most North American birds winter along the Pacific and Caribbean coasts of Mexico, Central America, and into South America, although a few winter along the west coast of United States (Poole *et al.*, 2002).

Habitats and Ecology: A pair of Ospreys nested near Big Horn for more than a decade until strong winds toppled the old cottonwood nest tree in 2014. Bighorn Audubon members erected two osprey platforms in 2015 on The Brinton grounds. From the 1950s to the 1970s Osprey populations crashed because of the use of the pesticide DDT, which reduced eggshell thickness and prevented hatching. The 1970s federal ban on DDT in the United States was a major factor in the population rebound of both Ospreys and Bald Eagles.

JAN	FEB	MAR	APR	MAY	JUNE	JULY	AUG	SEPT	OCT	NOV	DEC
			xxxx	xxxx	xxxx	xxxx	xxxx	xxxx	xxxx		

Bald Eagle (*Haliaeetus leucocephalus*)

Identification: Adult birds, with their white heads and tails, are unmistakable, but immatures are mostly brown and best distinguished from golden eagles by their relatively heavy bills and their underwing coverts, which are paler than their flight feathers. The legs and beaks are bright yellow. Young birds become sexually mature and have adult plumage by five years of age.

Voice: For such a large and powerful bird, male Bald Eagles have a rather timid-sounding call that is a rapid series of high-pitched piping notes. The female can respond with a single call note of similar frequency.

Status: Uncommon summer resident and common winter migrant.

Habitats and Ecology: This species feeds locally almost exclusively on carrion, particularly on road-killed deer, but in most regions it is a fish-eating species. In winter, watch for eagles just before dusk as they return to communal roost sites from their daily scavenging. Upward of twenty birds can be observed at The Brinton, perched in the large cottonwoods. Few eagles remain year-round, but some northern migrants spend the winter here and add to the local resident population (Faulkner, 2010).

JAN	FEB	MAR	APR	MAY	JUNE	JULY	AUG	SEPT	OCT	NOV	DEC
xxxx	xxxx	xxxx	xxxx	xxxx	xxxx	xxxx	xxx	xxx	xxxx	xxxx	xxxx

Cooper's Hawk (*Accipiter cooperii*)

Identification: Like other bird-eating (accipiter) hawks, this species is characterized by a long, rounded tail and broad, rounded wings that adapt it for rapid and maneuverable flying in forests. It is larger (crow-sized) than the Sharp-shinned Hawk and smaller than the elusive Northern Goshawk. Adults are blue-gray above with reddish barring on the chest and a narrow white terminal band on the tail. The rapid flap-flap-glide flight behavior of accipiter hawks is an aid to identification; most of the time the birds perch nearly invisibly in heavy vegetation, waiting for potential prey to appear, and then fly off the perch in high-speed pursuit.

Voice: The Cooper's Hawk is silent for much of the year, but during the breeding season both the male and female produce a *cak-cak-cak* alarm call in defense of the nest and during courtship. All three accipiter hawks have a very similar *cak* call type.

Status: Uncommon permanent resident.

Habitats and Ecology: This hawk is associated with mature forests, especially mixed or deciduous. Aspen groves are favored breeding locations. Like other accipiter hawks, it is a highly effective predator of birds up to about the size of a quail. A nesting pair on the Brinton Road produced young in consecutive years.

JAN	FEB	MAR	APR	MAY	JUNE	JULY	AUG	SEPT	OCT	NOV	DEC
xxxx	xxxx	xxxx	xxxx	xxxx	xxxx	xxxx	xxxx	xxxx	xxxx	xxxx	xxxx

Red-tailed Hawk (*Buteo jamaicensis*)

Identification: Red-tailed Hawk plumage is extremely variable, with many color forms ranging from light to very dark. The western race is darker with more streaking than the typical color form, which is a rich brown above and white below with a streaked belly or a variable belly-band of dark splotches. Buteos, in general, are distinguished from accipiters by their shorter tails and long, broad wings. The rusty tail of adults (visible only from above) is diagnostic, but immatures have brown-banded tails. Both age groups have blackish leading edges on their underwings, extending from the "armpit" to the "wrist," which is the best identifying characteristic in flight.

Voice: This familiar hawk makes a three-second *kee-eeee-rr* call, often heard while soaring.

Status: Common summer resident and migrant. Many Red-tailed Hawks migrate to the southern United States for the winter, although some winter in the area. Numbers vary, with peak migration in early April and October.

Habitats and Ecology: This is a common buteo hawk that occupies a broad range of habitats extending to open country, where nesting may occur on cliffs. However, trees, especially large cottonwoods and pines, are favored sites.

JAN	FEB	MAR	APR	MAY	JUNE	JULY	AUG	SEPT	OCT	NOV	DEC
x	xxxx	xxxx	xxxx	xxxx	xxxx	xxxx	xxxx	xxxx	xxxx	xx	x

Rough-legged Hawk (*Buteo lagopus*)

Identification: This large hawk has broad wings that appear long and narrow compared to those of other buteo hawks. It is called "rough-legged" because its tarsal feathers extend to the toes. There are many plumage variations between young and old, and degrees of overall melanism; however, all show dark "wrist" patches seen underneath the wings in flight, and all have white at the base of the tail and a dark tail tip. The breast is often heavily marked on a buffy background with a dark belly patch. These open-country hawks can often be seen hovering into the wind, a helpful identifying characteristic when they are seen flying. Their populations fluctuate in response to changes in abundance of prey—mostly small rodents—during their breeding season (Bechard and Swem, 2002).

Voice: The Rough-legged Hawk is in the region during winter, when it is mostly silent. During the Arctic breeding season, this hawk produces a catlike *mew* call.

Status: Common winter migrant that spends the breeding season on the northern Arctic tundra.

Habitats and Ecology: During the winter, this buteo prefers open grasslands, meadows, and croplands, habitats that are similar to its Arctic nesting environment. It also uses riparian areas adjacent to open country. Rough-legged Hawks have been found roosting in winter at The Brinton in the tall cottonwoods, sharing the riparian woods with Bald Eagles.

JAN	FEB	MAR	APR	MAY	JUNE	JULY	AUG	SEPT	OCT	NOV	DEC
xxxx	xxxx	xxxx	xxxx					xx	xxxx	xxxx	xxxx

Sandhill Crane (*Antigone canadensis*)

Identification: Sandhill Cranes are easily distinguished from all other local species except perhaps the larger herons; their grayish to rust-brown plumages and the bare red crowns of adults are distinctive, as is their goose-like manner of flying with the neck fully extended.

Voice: Mated pairs maintain their pair bonds with unison calling, which is a series of coordinated calls and distinctive posturing. While unison calling, both birds stand erect with heads thrown back and necks extended. The female utters two higher-pitched calls for each of the male's calls and simultaneously raises her beak to about 45 degrees above horizontal, while the male raises his to the vertical with each single-noted call.

Status: Common summer resident that winters in Bosque del Apache.

Habitats and Ecology: Sandhill Cranes are associated with wetlands, grasslands, and dense willow thickets along streams and near wetlands, where they often nest in reeds. Their average arrival in this region is March 17. The Rocky Mountain population of Greater Sandhill Cranes breeds throughout parts of Montana, Idaho, Wyoming, Nevada, Utah, and Colorado as well as farther west to the Cascades. About 20,000 birds, or more than 50 percent of the Rocky Mountain population, winter at the Bosque del Apache National Wildlife Refuge in New Mexico (Gerber *et al.*, 2014; Johnsgard, 2015a).

JAN	FEB	MAR	APR	MAY	JUNE	JULY	AUG	SEPT	OCT	NOV	DEC
		xx	xxxx	xxxx	xxxx	xxxx	xxxx	xxxx	xxxx	xxxx	

Killdeer (*Charadrius vociferus*)

Identification: The most widespread and common of the North American plovers, the Killdeer is easily recognized by its rusty brown tail and double breast band, together with its persistent calling, especially during the breeding season. Adults feign injury by performing "broken-wing" displays when their nest is threatened, effectively luring most intruders away.

Voice: An incessant *kill-dee* call, uttered mainly during the breeding season.

Status: The Killdeer is an abundant summer resident, sometimes overwintering, depending upon weather.

Habitats and Ecology: This species is widely distributed in open landscapes, including roadsides, reservoirs, ponds, gravel pits, golf courses, and suburban lawns. Gravelly areas with rocks about the size and color of the birds' eggs are favored. Nesting on rooftops sometimes occurs where gravelly habitats are absent. It forages visually on surface-dwelling insects, such as beetles, rather than probing for invisible foods in the manner of sandpipers and snipes.

JAN	FEB	MAR	APR	MAY	JUNE	JULY	AUG	SEPT	OCT	NOV	DEC
		xx	xxxx	xxxx	xxxx	xxxx	xxxx	xxxx	xx		

Eastern Screech-Owl (*Megascops asio*)

Identification: Screech-Owls are small, robin-sized, yellow-eyed owls with pointed ear-tufts and a grayish overall plumage that is strongly streaked and barred. This is the only local small owl with ear-tufts. Like other owls, the wings are rounded and the tail is short. The bill is greenish yellow in the eastern species; the Western Screech-Owl (*Megascops kennicottii*) has a blackish bill and is found in southwestern Wyoming.

Voice: The typical Eastern species' song is a whinny-like series of rising and falling soft trills uttered by both males and females.

Status: Uncommon permanent resident.

Habitats and Ecology: Associated with riparian cottonwood areas such as along Little Goose Creek, it prefers large, old trees that provide cavities for nesting, but it can also use nest boxes. Screech-Owls hide in trees during the day and become active at dusk. Both Eastern and Western Screech-Owls have been reported on Brinton Road, although the Eastern is the proven local breeder, and an adult was observed in a tree cavity at The Brinton in 2012. A rufous plumage variant of the Eastern species is present in western Nebraska and might rarely occur in eastern Wyoming.

JAN	FEB	MAR	APR	MAY	JUNE	JULY	AUG	SEPT	OCT	NOV	DEC
xxxx	xxxx	xxxx	xxxx	xxxx	xxxx	xxxx	xxxx	xxxx	xxxx	xxxx	xxxx

Great Horned Owl (*Bubo virginianus*)

Identification: The largest of the "eared" owls of the region, this species is one of the commonest. Up to two feet long, with wingspreads of almost four feet, only the rare Great Gray Owl (*Strix nebulosa*) is comparable in size, but it has a larger head that lacks ear-tufts. Owls have notably large eyes, with round pupils that open widely in the dark, and most species are specialized for night vision but lack color vision. Their heads can swivel 180 degrees, allowing their frontal facial disks to direct sound waves to their ears.

Voice: The usual call is a low hoot, *who-whoah-who, who-ah-whoo*.

Status: Common permanent resident.

Habitats and Ecology: A powerful and adaptable owl, this species occurs everywhere from riparian woodlands through the coniferous forest zones and into rocky canyons well away from trees. Nesting is thus highly variable but often occurs in abandoned bird or squirrel nests, on tree crotches or rock ledges, or rarely even on the ground. This species nests in the older large cottonwoods at The Brinton. Young have been produced in consecutive years.

JAN	FEB	MAR	APR	MAY	JUNE	JULY	AUG	SEPT	OCT	NOV	DEC
xxxx	xxxx	xxxx	xxxx	xxxx	xxxx	xxxx	xxxx	xxxx	xxxx	xxxx	xxxx

Broad-tailed Hummingbird (*Selasphorus platycercus*)

Identification: Adult males have a ruby-red gorget and a white crescent behind the eye. The underparts are white, with metallic green sides. When perched, the longest primaries do not extend beyond the long, relatively broad tail. Females and immatures have slightly speckled white throats, pale cinnamon flanks, and some rufous on the outer tail feathers. Males are distinguished from the smaller and more common Calliope Hummingbird by their more rounded and entirely red gorget.

Voice: Males produce a loud and buzzy insect-like trill generated by their wings while in flight.

Status: A common summer resident, it winters in western Mexico and Central America.

Habitats and Ecology: A hummingbird of subalpine meadows, it ranges across the south-central Rockies in summer. It possesses a number of physiological and behavioral adaptations to survive cold nights, including an ability to enter overnight torpor, slowing its heart rate and dropping its body temperature. The selection of a nest site under a tree canopy might keep the nighttime temperatures it experiences warmer, and their tiny nests are placed so as to receive early morning sunlight. Hummingbirds have extremely high metabolic rates and consume approximately their body weight equivalent in nectar daily (Erlich *et al.*, 1988; Johnsgard, 1997).

JAN	FEB	MAR	APR	MAY	JUNE	JULY	AUG	SEPT	OCT	NOV	DEC
				xxxx	xxxx	xxxx	xxxx	xxxx			

Calliope Hummingbird (*Selasphorus calliope*)

Identification: This species is the smallest (3 inches) long-distance avian migrant in the world, breeding north to British Columbia, wintering in Mexico, and traveling up to 5,600 miles annually on its round-trip migrations (Calder and Calder, 1994). It has a comparatively short tail and bill; its longest primary tips extend past the end of the tail when perched. Adult males are unique in having an elongated gorget of iridescent magenta heavily streaked with white. Females and immatures are best recognized by their tiny size, a slightly streaked white throat, and pale cinnamon flanks.

Voice: Hummingbirds are named for the distinctive "humming" sound produced by their wings. The Calliope makes a light *chip* and a high-frequency *squeak* while feeding. The male display call is a high-pitched single *zee-ree* note.

Status: A common summer resident, it winters in the southern states and Mexico, although wintering has become increasingly common in the south-central United States (Calder and Calder, 1994; Johnsgard, 1997).

Habitats and Ecology: This species prefers open meadow areas near coniferous forests, especially low willow or sage areas rich in nectar-producing plants, such as paintbrush and gilia. Openings in woodlands, sometimes as high as timberline, are also frequented, and in late summer, alpine meadows are preferred by migrating birds. The Calliope is common at The Brinton's urban gardens in summer.

JAN	FEB	MAR	APR	MAY	JUNE	JULY	AUG	SEPT	OCT	NOV	DEC
				xxxx	xxxx	xxxx	xxxx	x			

Belted Kingfisher (*Megaceryle alcyon*)

Identification: This large (13 inches) and conspicuous bird is easily identified by a bluish crested head, a wide bluish upper breast-band, and white underparts. Females have a second rufous band across the lower breast that is separated from the anterior band by white. Kingfishers are always found near water and often hover above its surface, sometimes followed by a plunge into it to capture prey.

Voice: In flight, kingfishers utter a dry rattling call that resembles the sound of a fishing reel, which is often heard along Little Goose Creek, even in winter when open water is available.

Status: Common permanent resident.

Habitats and Ecology: This species is found near water that is rich in fish populations, usually where nearby roadcuts, eroded banks, gravel pits, or other steep earthen exposures provide opportunities for excavating earthen tunnel nests, and also where nearby tree branches provide convenient perching and observation sites. Undigested fish remains are regurgitated and can often be found near perching places. These birds typically choose nesting sites along streams where there are riffles that provide habitat for the small fish they prey upon (Ehrlich *et al.*, 1988).

JAN	FEB	MAR	APR	MAY	JUNE	JULY	AUG	SEPT	OCT	NOV	DEC
xxxx	xxxx	xxxx	xxxx	xxxx	xxxx	xxxx	xxxx	xxxx	xxxx	xxxx	xxxx

Downy Woodpecker (*Picoides pubescens*)

Identification: This species closely resembles the Hairy Woodpecker (*Picoides villosis*) but is smaller (7 versus 9 inches) and has a shorter and more slender beak that is about half as long as the head. Like the less common Hairy Woodpecker, both sexes are mostly black and white, with extensive white on the back and rump, and white spotting on the wings. Males have a small red nape patch.

Voice: Woodpeckers don't sing, but they do have loud calls. The species' call is a high whinny descending in pitch and a sharp *pik*. They often drum against wood or metal, the noise having the same territorial-proclamation effect as the songs of other birds.

Status: Common permanent resident.

Habitats and Ecology: A wide variety of wooded habitats are used by this species, but it has a preference for open deciduous riparian woodlands. Downy Woodpeckers favor nesting in cottonwoods on the plains and prefer aspens in the mountains. Both males and females participate in excavating a nest cavity with an entrance about an inch wide and a cavity 6 to 12 inches deep (Jackson and Ouellet, 2002). Woodpeckers are called "primary excavators" because of their ability to excavate nest holes in trees that are used secondarily by several other species, including the Black-capped Chickadee, American Kestrel, and Eastern Screech-Owl.

JAN	FEB	MAR	APR	MAY	JUNE	JULY	AUG	SEPT	OCT	NOV	DEC
xxxx	xxxx	xxxx	xxxx	xxxx	xxxx	xxxx	xxxx	xxxx	xxxx	xxxx	xxxx

Red-naped Sapsucker (*Sphyrapicus nuchalis*)

Identification: A medium-sized woodpecker with a bright red crown in both sexes, the male Red-naped Sapsucker has a red throat and chin while the female has a white chin and less red on the throat. Both sexes and the more brownish immatures have large white wing-patches, spotted to barred backs, and buffy to white underparts.

Voice: A repetitive beak-drumming is a common clue to a territorial male. When parents are not at the nest, chicks vocalize constantly.

Status: A common summer resident, it winters in Mexico and the southern United States (Walters *et al.*, 2014).

Habitats and Ecology: Red-naped Sapsuckers breed in aspen groves and deciduous forests as well as open ponderosa pine forests at lower elevations in the Rocky Mountains. These birds are specialized for obtaining sap with their specialized tongues, thus the name "sapsucker." To extract sap, they drill a series of shallow, evenly spaced holes in the bark of various sap-producing trees, often aspens or poplars. Hummingbirds and other species also feed from both the sap wells and on the insects that the sap attracts. Sapsuckers excavate new nesting holes each year, so the previous year's nest holes become available for secondary cavity nesters of similar size, such as the Red-breasted Nuthatch and Mountain Chickadee (Ehrlich *et al.*, 1988).

JAN	FEB	MAR	APR	MAY	JUNE	JULY	AUG	SEPT	OCT	NOV	DEC
			xxx	xxxx	xxxx	xxxx	xxxx	xxxx	x		

Northern Flicker (*Colaptes auratus*)

Identification: This woodpecker is mostly barred brown with black-scalloped patterning, a black breast-band, and underparts spotted heavily with black. A white rump patch is visible in flight. Red malar (moustache) stripes are present in males of the western subspecies (*C. a. cafer*), which also have salmon-red tints on the undersides of their wing and tail feathers. The eastern subspecies (*C. a. auritus*) is yellow in tint on these feathers, and males have black malar stripes. Intermediate-colored hybrids often occur where the two races are in contact, particularly east of the Bighorn Mountains.

Voice: Vocalizations include a *wick-a-wick-a-wick-a*, heard on breeding grounds, and a *klee-yer* that is uttered year-round (Wiebe and Moore, 2008).

Status: The Northern Flicker is a common permanent resident, but some altitudinal movements from the Rocky Mountains into the Great Plains occur.

Habitats and Ecology: Broadly distributed, Flickers are unusual among woodpeckers because much of their food consists of insects, such as ants and beetles, that are obtained by probing in the ground. Flickers are often found in cottonwoods and riparian zones where snags are present. There they excavate nest holes that later become available for other cavity-nesting species.

JAN	FEB	MAR	APR	MAY	JUNE	JULY	AUG	SEPT	OCT	NOV	DEC
xxxx	xxxx	xxxx	xxxx	xxxx	xxxx	xxxx	xxxx	xxxx	xxxx	xxxx	xxxx

American Kestrel (*Falco sparverius*)

Identification: This tiny (10-inch) falcon, previously known as the Sparrow Hawk, may commonly be observed perched on telephone wires, where it often bobs its tail, or in flight, where it might be hovering above possible prey. Males have a rusty back and tail, a conspicuous black "mustache" of two black stripes on a white face, and bluish gray wings. Females are more brownish overall and have a brownish barred tail.

Voice: A shrill chittering disturbance call, *killy killy killy*, is uttered by both sexes.

Status: The Kestrel is a common summer resident, and some birds overwinter during mild years.

Habitats and Ecology: This is an open-country falcon that nests in tree cavities previously excavated by woodpeckers, or in natural cavities of large trees. A pair successfully nested at The Brinton in a large cottonwood in 2015, producing five young.

JAN	FEB	MAR	APR	MAY	JUNE	JULY	AUG	SEPT	OCT	NOV	DEC
xxxx	xxxx	xxxx	xxxx	xxxx	xxxx	xxxx	xxxx	xxxx	xxxx	xxxx	xxxx

Western Wood-Pewee (*Contopus sordidulus*)

Identification: This inconspicuous brownish flycatcher is much more likely to be heard than seen. If seen, the generally dark grayish brown upperparts, without strong wing-barring or a definite pale eye-ring, help to identify it. Their foraging behavior also helps identify most flycatchers as such because they sally off favorite perches in pursuit of insects and then return to the same perch.

Voice: A descending *pee-er* and *pzzeeyeer* is uttered during the day and also as the dawn song. The *pee-er* song can often be heard from high perches within the male's territory (Bemis and Rising, 1999).

Status: A common summer resident, it winters in South America.

Habitats and Ecology: Wood-pewees breed in most coniferous forest types and also to varying extent in aspens, riparian forests, and various open deciduous or mixed woodland habitats. Open forests are favored, especially those dominated by conifers. Nests are built on horizontal branches of trees, or sometimes on a fork, and are usually well covered with spider webs, to which lichens may be attached for camouflage.

JAN	FEB	MAR	APR	MAY	JUNE	JULY	AUG	SEPT	OCT	NOV	DEC
				xx	xxxx	xxxx	xxxx	xx			

Say's Phoebe (*Sayornis saya*)

Identification: This is a medium-sized flycatcher with a dusky gray-brown back and tinting of rusty brown on the lower breast and belly. The brownish black tail is often pumped up and down. When feeding, the Say's Phoebe usually captures flying insects from a perch, often returning to the same perch. The species can also frequently be seen hover-gleaning insects from the ground.

Voice: The male's primary song is series of repeated vocalizations: *pit-tsee-eur* and *pit eet*. A *phee-eur* call is commonly used in many situations by both sexes (Schukman and Wolf, 1998).

Status: A common summer resident, it winters from the southwestern United States to central Mexico.

Habitats and ecology: These birds are found in rather dry habitats, where their brownish earth colors seem especially appropriate. They often occupy canyons, open grasslands, sagebrush, and mountain foothills. Frequently, they nest on human structures.

JAN	FEB	MAR	APR	MAY	JUNE	JULY	AUG	SEPT	OCT	NOV	DEC
			xxxx	xxxx	xxxx	xxxx	xxxx	xxxx			

Eastern Kingbird (*Tyrannus tyrannus*)

Identification: *Tyrannus* means "tyrant" in Latin and is descriptive of the tyrannids' aggressive defense of their territory and mate. Kingbirds are commonly seen in summer hawking insects in Brinton open spaces. The Eastern species' plumage is black above and white below, with a broad white tail tip that is easily visible in flight, whereas the more yellowish gray Western species has white outer tail feathers.

Voice: The territorial song is a long series of chits and twitters. This kingbird is one of the noisiest small birds of the region, and from the time of its arrival until nesting is well underway its screaming calls and chases of other birds are often evident.

Status: A common summer resident, it winters in South America, mainly in the western Amazonian basin.

Habitats and Ecology: The Eastern Kingbird is associated with open areas that have scattered trees or tall shrubs, such as forest edges, fencerows, riparian areas, and agricultural lands.

JAN	FEB	MAR	APR	MAY	JUNE	JULY	AUG	SEPT	OCT	NOV	DEC
				xxxx	xxxx	xxxx	xxxx	xx			

Black-billed Magpie (*Pica hudsonia*)

Identification: Magpies are easily identified by their long, pointed tails, black-and-white body plumage, and black wings with flashing white inner markings that are exposed in flight. These social birds have adapted to humans and were observed following hunting parties of the Plains tribes by Lewis and Clark (Trost, 1999).

Voice: Very noisy birds, the magpies have a chattering call of *wock, wock, wock-a-wock* and a raspy chatter.

Status: The Black-billed Magpie is a common local permanent resident, but the species is declining nationally as a result of West Nile disease.

Habitats and Ecology: Of widespread occurrence, it is most common in riparian areas with thicket vegetation, sagebrush, aspen groves, and the lower coniferous forest zones. Especially favored magpie nest sites are small, thorny trees, in which they build large stick and mud nests covered by a protective dome. Old nests are often used for shelter during bad weather by smaller birds such as robins and blackbirds, and small owls are known to have used these structures for roosting during daytime (Bent, 1946).

JAN	FEB	MAR	APR	MAY	JUNE	JULY	AUG	SEPT	OCT	NOV	DEC
xxxx	xxxx	xxxx	xxxx	xxxx	xxxx	xxxx	xxxx	xxxx	xxxx	xxxx	xxxx

American Crow (*Corvus brachyrhynchos*)

Identification: This familiar bird is medium sized and black plumaged, and can be distinguished from the similar Common Raven by its smaller size and rounded tail, as compared with the wedge-shaped tail of the raven. The crow's beak is also noticeably both shorter and less robust than the raven's (Ehrlich *et al.*, 1988). Crows are often found in small groups, whereas ravens are rather solitary, traveling in pairs.

Voice: The crow is very vocal, with many distinct vocalizations. The familiar *caw* is the primary call used for long-distance communication. This call can be short, medium, or long in duration. Crow calls exhibit variations among birds that may help identify individuals (Reaume, 1988).

Status: Common permanent resident.

Habitats and Ecology: Of widespread occurrence, crows prefer open habitats for feeding, with scattered trees for roosting. Crows are omnivorous and usually forage on the ground.

JAN	FEB	MAR	APR	MAY	JUNE	JULY	AUG	SEPT	OCT	NOV	DEC
xxxx	xxxx	xxxx	xxxx	xxxx	xxxx	xxxx	xxxx	xxxx	xxxx	xxxx	xxxx

Common Raven (*Corvus corax*)

Identification: This species is the largest of all passerine (perching) birds. It is uniformly lustrous black and can be distinguished from the American Crow by its larger body size, wedge-shaped tail, and heavier bill. In flight, the Common Raven's outer wing feathers exhibit longer, more widely separated "fingers" at their tips. Ravens are usually observed singly or in pairs.

Voice: The raven's low-frequency deep *caw* call is audible for long distances. Sometimes ravens mimic the calls of other birds; recent evidence suggests that the number of call types could be limitless because of regional dialects and the variations in individual raven calls (Boarman and Heinrich, 1999).

Status: Uncommon permanent resident.

Habitats and Ecology: Ravens occur in nearly all habitats and have adapted to human environments. They typically gather in communal night roosts when not nesting, and they are omnivorous, eating carrion, bird eggs, fish, and large insects. Ravens are known to be extremely intelligent. Their play behavior is well documented, such as the dropping and aerial catching of objects and social "tug of war." The oldest known documented survival record in the wild was 22 years (Boarman and Heinrich, 1999).

JAN	FEB	MAR	APR	MAY	JUNE	JULY	AUG	SEPT	OCT	NOV	DEC
xxxx	xxxx	xxxx	xxxx	xxxx	xxxx	xxxx	xxxx	xxxx	xxxx	xxxx	xxxx

Tree Swallow (*Tachycineta bicolor*)

Identification: This attractive swallow is a two-toned iridescent bluish black above and immaculate white below, and has a somewhat forked tail. It closely resembles the Violet-green Swallow but lacks that western species' large white flank patches.

Voice: Both males and females of this species sing a high-pitched and liquid *chirp* and *gurgle*. Their calls, similar to their songs, are a series of chirps but also include ticking sounds and chatters.

Status: A common summer resident, it winters in Mexico and Central America. It is the earliest local swallow to return north in spring to its breeding grounds.

Habitats and Ecology: Breeding in the region extends from riparian woodlands through the aspen zone and into a variety of open habitats like fields and wetlands. Outside the breeding season they are often seen over lakes and rivers, where they frequently form huge flocks. Nesting is common in aspen groves, where old woodpecker holes are available, but they also nest in birdhouses. At times a male may support two mates in separate nest sites, and reportedly even three birds may build a nest, incubate the eggs, and feed the young (Bent, 1942).

JAN	FEB	MAR	APR	MAY	JUNE	JULY	AUG	SEPT	OCT	NOV	DEC
		x	xxxx	xxxx	xxxx	xxxx	xxxx	x			

Cliff Swallow (*Petrochelidon pyrrhonota*)

Identification: The Cliff Swallow is easily recognized by its golden-orange rump patch, square rather than forked tail, and a yellowish white forehead patch. It is a highly social species and is usually seen in large groups on the breeding grounds where it nests in colonies of up to thousands of pairs.

Voice: The song is a series of squeaks, while the call is a soft *chur*, both heard during the breeding season. They also produce a chattering flock call and an alarm call, used in their dense colonies, where nests are crowded closely together.

Status: An abundant summer resident, it winters in South America. Cliff Swallows are often seen in large numbers as they congregate during peak migration in mid to late August.

Habitats and Ecology: A wide variety of nesting areas are used by this species, but in the Bighorn Mountains region, vertical cliff sides below 9,000 feet elevation are preferred nest sites (Faulkner, 2010). With the advent of roads and human infrastructure, Cliff Swallows have adopted bridges, overpasses, and barns as their favored colonial nesting sites. The nests are gourd-like structures of dried mud, built from small mud globules that are gathered by the birds and carried back in the bill. These birds are even known to carry their eggs in their beaks to place them in the nests of other individuals, performing a unique form of brood parasitism (Brown and Brown, 1988).

JAN	FEB	MAR	APR	MAY	JUNE	JULY	AUG	SEPT	OCT	NOV	DEC
			xx	xxxx	xxxx	xxxx	xxxx	xxx			

Black-capped Chickadee (*Poecile atricapillus*)

Identification: The Black-capped Chickadee is a tiny songbird with a large head and short body, resulting in a rotund body shape. The cap and bib are black, the cheeks are white, the back is gray, the breast whitish with buffy sides, and the inner wing feathers are edged with white. The black cap extends down to just beyond the eyes, nearly hiding them from view.

Voice: Adults have about 16 distinct vocalizations that communicate information to mates and neighbors (Smith, 1991). The species' familiar *chickadee-dee-dee* call is uttered year-round. The male's typical spring song is a melodic *fee-bee* that advertises territories and attracts mates. There are also gargling noises and notes that announce aerial predators and coordinate winter flock movements (Foote *et al.*, 2010).

Status: Common permanent resident.

Habitats and Ecology: Chickadees prefer open coniferous forests, especially pines. Woodpecker holes or self-excavated cavities in rotted wood are used for nesting. Aspen groves and riparian woodlands are favorite habitats. Pair bonds dissolve in winter, when flocking occurs, and birds often gather at feeders.

JAN	FEB	MAR	APR	MAY	JUNE	JULY	AUG	SEPT	OCT	NOV	DEC
xxxx	xxxx	xxxx	xxxx	xxxx	xxxx	xxxx	xxxx	xxxx	xxxx	xxxx	xxxx

Mountain Chickadee (*Poecile gambeli*)

Identification: The Mountain Chickadee resembles the Black-capped Chickadee, but the white facial marks are interrupted by a black line extending from the nape forward through the eye region.

Voice: The male's song is nearly the same as that of the Black-capped Chickadee, but the typical call is usually a three- or four-note descending whistle, sometimes described as very raspy.

Status: Common permanent resident.

Habitats and Ecology: This chickadee is a permanent resident of high-elevation mature coniferous forests up to timberline, where it caches conifer seeds in autumn. It often joins mixed flocks of kinglets and nuthatches. Old woodpecker holes are often used for nesting. Populations locally migrate to exploit geographic variations in seed abundance (McCallum *et al.*, 1999).

JAN	FEB	MAR	APR	MAY	JUNE	JULY	AUG	SEPT	OCT	NOV	DEC
xxxx	xxxx	xxxx	xxxx	xxxx	xxxx	xxxx	xxxx	xxxx	xxxx	xxxx	xxxx

Red-breasted Nuthatch (*Sitta canadensis*)

Identification: This small nuthatch (4 inches long) is the only North American species of the group that has a distinct black line extending back from the eye, in the same manner as occurs in the Mountain Chickadee. Males also have reddish brown flanks, but these are rather obscure in females. It is distinguished from the White-breasted Nuthatch by both its breast color and black eye-line.

Voice: The species' call is a nasal *yank yank*, often repeated. The name "nuthatch" is an early English variant of "nut-hacker," referring to the bird's ability to peck open shelled seeds.

Status: Common permanent resident.

Habitats and Ecology: This nuthatch has a preference for coniferous forests, especially fir and spruce, and deciduous forests, across a wide range of elevations. Western populations prefer high tree canopies and large trees (Ghalambor and Martin, 1999). Cavity nesting occurs in the trunks of dead trees or the rotting portion of live trees. The birds typically excavate their own nesting holes, lining the opening with sticky resin that might help repel intruders. These tiny nuthatches sometimes undertake long-distance irruptive movements in search of food.

JAN	FEB	MAR	APR	MAY	JUNE	JULY	AUG	SEPT	OCT	NOV	DEC
xxxx	xxxx	xxxx	xxxx	xxxx	xxxx	xxxx	xxxx	xxxx	xxxx	xxxx	xxxx

Brown Creeper (*Certhia americana*)

Identification: This well-camouflaged bird is aptly named because it forages while creeping along tree bark, using its long spine-tipped tail as a prop while climbing the trunks. It has a long, narrow, and slightly decurved bill and a buffy stripe over the eye. Creepers climb up tree trunks, picking up food in the crevices of bark along their path, whereas nuthatches move downward over tree surfaces in their food search.

Voice: The males' very high-frequency song sounds like "*Trees, beautiful trees.*" Creepers also utter a call that is similar in its high frequencies to the Golden-crowned Kinglet (*Regulus satrapa*) call.

Status: Uncommon permanent resident.

Habitats and Ecology: The local presence of creepers is indicative of forest ecosystem health. Creepers select the oldest and largest trees having thick, grooved bark with crevices to probe for insects. Nests are placed virtually invisibly in crevices, typically behind a loosened flap of bark.

JAN	FEB	MAR	APR	MAY	JUNE	JULY	AUG	SEPT	OCT	NOV	DEC
xxxx	xxxx	xxxx	xxxx	xxxx	xxxx	xxxx	xxxx	xxxx	xxxx	xxxx	xxxx

House Wren (*Troglodytes aedon*)

Identification: This familiar wren was named for its tendency to nest around houses or in birdhouses. The overall brownish plumage has few field marks, except for a faint superciliary line.

Voice: This wren's complex song is a string of intense and boisterous rapidly rising and falling notes. Rendall and Kaluthota (2013) found that one male uttered 194 different song variants. Early in the breeding season, females also utter a much simpler song that sounds like a human squeal (L. S. Johnson, personal communication).

Status: The House Wren is a common summer resident that winters in the southern United States and Mexico.

Habitats and Ecology: Wrens breed in a wide variety of semi-open habitats, especially deciduous woodlands with snags. Natural holes in trees, nest boxes, and a wide variety of other cavities are used for nesting in urban landscapes. House wrens are generally not found in contiguous forests but instead prefer forests thinned by fire, defoliation by insects, or human activity (Johnson, 2014). Polygamous mating is common in the population that occupies The Brinton grounds, which was the subject of intensive ornithological research in the 1980s and 1990s (L. S. Johnson, personal communication).

JAN	FEB	MAR	APR	MAY	JUNE	JULY	AUG	SEPT	OCT	NOV	DEC
			x	xxxx	xxxx	xxxx	xxxx	xxxx			

American Dipper (*Cinclus mexicanus*)

Identification: Easily identified, the American Dipper is confined to mountain streams and resembles an overgrown wren but is uniformly gray and has a short cocked tail. The common name "dipper" recalls the species' distinctive bobbing up-and-down behavior.

Voice: The male's territorial song is loud, melodious, and bubbling, much like a House Wren's.

Status: Common permanent resident.

Habitats and Ecology: This species is found on rapidly flowing mountain streams, often with waterfalls or cascades present. John Muir described their close association as "bird and stream . . . inseparable" (Muir, 1894). Dippers select clear, clean, and cold water, and their presence can be used to assess a stream's water quality. Foraging for invertebrates is done underwater by diving, often in rushing streams. Dippers have special oxygen-carrying blood cells that adapt them to survive the cold water of mountain streams. Nests are sometimes attached to rock walls or overhangs or tucked behind waterfalls or under bridges. Dippers have regularly nested beneath the small bridge leading to the Brinton horse barn.

JAN	FEB	MAR	APR	MAY	JUNE	JULY	AUG	SEPT	OCT	NOV	DEC
xxxx	xxxx	xxxx	xxxx	xxxx	xxxx	xxxx	xxxx	xxxx	xxxx	xxxx	xxxx

Mountain Bluebird (*Sialia currucoides*)

Identification: Male Mountain Bluebirds are the only birds of the region that have cerulean blue upperparts and pale blue underparts. Females are mostly grayish brown above and below but exhibit blue coloration on the wing and rump. Bluebirds forage for ground-dwelling insects from perches and often hover kestrel-like above prey.

Voice: The species' primary territorial song is often begun long before dawn and is a repetitive warble, similar to the American Robin's.

Status: The Mountain Bluebird is a common summer resident at or above 4,700 feet, very rare below 4,400 feet, and sparse in between (L. S. Johnson, personal communication, December 7, 2016). They are present nearly throughout the year, although migrants sometimes winter as far south as central Mexico.

Habitats and Ecology: Breeding occurs in open woodlands and forest-edge habitats from mountain meadows downward through the ponderosa pine zone and into the aspen zone. Nesting occurs either where dead trees are available for nest cavities, or where rock crevices are present. "Extramarital affairs" are common in the local population, with females preferring to mate with the most intensely colored males, especially if their own mates are relatively dull (L. S. Johnson, personal communication).

JAN	FEB	MAR	APR	MAY	JUNE	JULY	AUG	SEPT	OCT	NOV	DEC
		xxxx	xxxx	xxxx	xxxx	xxxx	xxxx	xxxx	xxxx		

Cedar Waxwing (*Bombycilla cedrorum*)

Identification: "Waxwing" refers to the red tips of the secondary flight feathers, which resemble drops of sealing wax and are present on adults of both sexes. This species closely resembles the commonly overwintering Bohemian Waxwing but lacks white wing markings and has gray rather than chestnut under-tail coverts and a breast that is distinctly yellow rather than gray. Adults of both species have a black facial mask; relatively long, pointed wings; and a black tail with a yellow terminal band.

Voice: The most commonly heard vocalization is a very high frequency *seee*.

Status: Common permanent resident.

Habitats and Ecology: Open woodlands, primarily of broad-leaved species, are used for nesting, including riparian forests. Locally, areas that have abundant fruiting plants, such as juniper and crabapples are especially favored, although insects, buds, and other food sources are also consumed. During winter in the Bighorn Mountains region, this highly mobile species joins large, highly social flocks of Bohemian Waxwings in search of persistent berries. Because of their preference for berries and other fruits, waxwings are important dispersers of fruiting plants and ensure the continuity of the habitats on which they depend (Witmer *et al.*, 2014).

JAN	FEB	MAR	APR	MAY	JUNE	JULY	AUG	SEPT	OCT	NOV	DEC
xxxx	xxxx	xxxx	xxxx	xxxx	xxxx	xxxx	xxxx	xxxx	xxxx	xxxx	xxxx

Yellow Warbler (*Setophaga petechia*)

Identification: This species is the most uniformly bright yellow of all the regional warblers, with a special fondness for foraging in willows (*Salix* spp.). Males have a series of reddish brown breast streaks, while females are generally duller and more olive throughout, with only faint brownish chest streaking.

Voice: The song is a distinctive *tseet-tseet-tseet-sitta-sitta-see* or "*sweet, sweet, sweet—oh so sweet.*"

Status: The Yellow Warbler is a common summer resident, wintering southward to Central and South America.

Habitats and Ecology: Yellow Warblers prefer moist habitats such as riparian woodlands and brushy, wet, deciduous thickets, with a preference for willows. Nests are built in the forks of bushes or trees. Brown-headed Cowbirds (*Molothrus ater*) are a frequent brood parasite of this warbler, although the warblers may roof over a parasitized nest and begin a new clutch.

JAN	FEB	MAR	APR	MAY	JUNE	JULY	AUG	SEPT	OCT	NOV	DEC
				xxxx	xxxx	xxxx	xxxx	xxx			

Yellow-rumped Warbler (*Setophaga coronata*)

Identification: Formerly considered two species—the Myrtle (*S. c. coronata*) in eastern North America and the Audubon's (*S. c. auduboni*) in the American West—this
now-single species is named for its yellow rump. Males of *auduboni* have a distinctive combination of yellow rump, flank patch, crown, and throat but otherwise are
mostly bluish gray above and white below. Females also have yellow rumps and
flank markings but otherwise are rather dull in color. Males of *coronata* are similar
to *auduboni*, but their throat color is white rather than yellow.

Voice: The primary male song is a soft warble that changes in pitch toward the end.

Status: A common summer resident, the Yellow-rumped is rare or absent in winter when
the birds travel south to the southern United States or Mexico for winter plant foods.

Habitats and Ecology: This species breeds predominantly in mature coniferous forests
and mixed coniferous-deciduous habitats, and occurs at all elevations in the Bighorn Mountains region. It forages from low branches to the highest crown levels.
The birds are often seen fluttering out from a tree to catch insects. On migration
and during winter, they eat fruits and berries that among warblers they are notably
able to digest. This adaptation allows them to winter farther north than other North
American warblers (Hunt and Flaspohler, 1998).

JAN	FEB	MAR	APR	MAY	JUNE	JULY	AUG	SEPT	OCT	NOV	DEC
			xx	xxxx	xxxx	xxxx	xxxx	xxxx	xxx		

Spotted Towhee (*Pipilo maculatus*)

Identification: The general term "sparrow" includes dozens of small New World and Old World seed-eating and ground-foraging species. The Spotted Towhee is a large sparrow, easily identified by a black (males) or brown (females) head and breast that resembles a hood, a white-spotted black back, a long black tail, and chestnut flanks. The related eastern form, the Eastern Towhee (*Pipilo erythropthalmus*), lacks white back spots. Hybrids that have only slight white spotting might occasionally occur in eastern Wyoming.

Voice: The male's primary song is a variable version of the Eastern species' *Drink-your-tea*. Early in the breeding season, territorial males sing about 80 percent of the daylight hours (Greenlaw, 1996). The Spotted Towhee's call is a nasal and cat-like *wheee* or *chee-ee*, much like the Eastern species' *tow-eee* call.

Status: A common summer resident, it winters in the southern United States and Mexico.

Habitat and Ecology: This is a ground-adapted sparrow that breeds in a wide variety of plant associations. It requires a low, dense, and brushy component with an accumulation of litter and humus, and a protective overhead screen of shrubby foliage. It prefers riparian areas, foothill shrublands, and lower-elevation ponderosa pine forests. It is most often seen on the ground, foraging in leaf litter for insects and plants (Bartos and Greenlaw, 2015).

JAN	FEB	MAR	APR	MAY	JUNE	JULY	AUG	SEPT	OCT	NOV	DEC
			xx	xxxx	xxxx	xxxx	xxxx	xxxx	xx		

Vesper Sparrow (*Pooecetes gramineus*)

Identification: This is the only pale-colored, medium-large grassland sparrow with white outer tail feathers. The adult sexes are alike, with conspicuous whitish eye-rings and a weakly streaked breast that sometimes forms a central spot. Unlike the similar Savannah Sparrow (*Passerculus sandwichensis*) and Song Sparrow (*Melospiza melodea*), the Vesper Sparrow has a paler back, chestnut patches on the upper-wing coverts, and a white-edged tail.

Voice: This species' song is musical and somewhat like that of a Song Sparrow but usually has two pairs of preliminary slurred notes followed by a descending trill: *Here, here; where-where; all together down the hill.* Males often sing in early evening, thus the name Vesper Sparrow.

Status: An abundant summer resident, it winters from the southern United States to Mexico.

Habitats and Ecology: Breeding occurs in dry, open habitats with short vegetation such as native shortgrass prairie, sagebrush steppe, pastures, and hayfields with low to moderate shrub and forb cover. Wet areas with tall vegetation are avoided (Jones and Cornely, 2002).

JAN	FEB	MAR	APR	MAY	JUNE	JULY	AUG	SEPT	OCT	NOV	DEC
			xxx	xxxx	xxxx	xxxx	xxxx	xxxx	xx		

Dark-eyed Junco (*Junco hyemalis*)

Identification: This bird is a common and familiar "snowbird" that shows marked geographical variation in plumage coloration that ranges geographically from being mostly black to dark grayish ("slate-colored" race) above, to having a pearly gray head with a bluish gray cast and pinkish cinnamon flanks ("pink-sided" race). Formerly regarded as consisting of five distinct species, all are now considered a single species collectively named the Dark-eyed Junco (Nolan *et al.*, 2002). The pink-sided race is a common breeder in the Bighorn Mountains and the north-central Rockies. The outer tail feathers of all races are white, and those in the center are blackish, which is evident in flight.

Voice: The males' song is a series of musical trills of the same pitch, resembling that of a Chipping Sparrow (*Spizella passerina*).

Status: A common permanent resident, it descends in elevation during winter, when the birds form foraging flocks at local feeders.

Habitats and Ecology: These sparrows prefer montane forests and aspen groves with a dense understory and plants that provide cover for their ground nests, but they sometimes nest in a small cavity or hole on a mountain rock face (Faulkner, 2010; Nolan *et al.*, 2002). They primarily feed on seeds and insects, scratching on the ground and among underbrush.

JAN	FEB	MAR	APR	MAY	JUNE	JULY	AUG	SEPT	OCT	NOV	DEC
xxxx	xxxx	xxxx	xxxx	xxxx	xxxx	xxxx	xxxx	xxxx	xxxx	xxxx	xxxx

Western Tanager (*Piranga ludoviciana*)

Identification: The male of this handsome western songbird is lemon yellow with coal-black wings, back, and tail and an orange-red head during the spring and summer. The female is much duller: mostly yellow below with a greenish yellow back and a black tail and wings, the latter crossed by two white wing-bars.

Voice: The male's song is like that of the American Robin but more hoarse, consisting of two- and three-syllable notes. Because it is often inconspicuous from its preferred position in tree canopies, its song is useful in field identification of this species.

Status: A common summer resident, it winters from Mexico to Costa Rica.

Habitats and Ecology: During breeding, the Western Tanager ranges farther north than other tanagers—as far as northern Canada, where it breeds in open and mixed coniferous and deciduous forests and riparian forests. It is common in low- to mid-elevation forests, foraging on insects and fruits such as wild cherries, elderberries, and serviceberries (Hudson, 1999).

JAN	FEB	MAR	APR	MAY	JUNE	JULY	AUG	SEPT	OCT	NOV	DEC
				xx	xxxx	xxxx	xxxx	xxx			

Black-headed Grosbeak (*Pheucticus melanocephalus*)

Identification: Males of this large-beaked species are distinctively patterned with orange-yellow underparts and a black head, wings, and tail; the wings and tail are also variously spotted or striped with white. It is sometimes confused with the Evening Grosbeak (*Coccothraustes vespertinus*), but that species has more bright yellow on the back and underparts, and a bright yellow forehead. The female Black-headed Grosbeak is a chunky sparrow-like bird, with heavy dark cheek markings and a yellowish tinge on the underwings and belly.

Voice: The male's song is very similar to that of the American Robin in being melodious with a series of rapidly ascending and descending notes separated by brief pauses. Females sometimes also sing.

Status: A common summer resident, it winters in Mexico.

Habitats and Ecology: During the breeding season, this species is associated with deciduous woodlands that have fairly well-developed shrubby understories. It also occurs in a variety of habitats, including riparian zones, mountain foothills, aspen, ponderosa pine, and urban areas (Faulkner, 2010).

JAN	FEB	MAR	APR	MAY	JUNE	JULY	AUG	SEPT	OCT	NOV	DEC
				xxxx	xxxx	xxxx	xxxx	xx			

Lazuli Bunting (*Passerina amoena*)

Identification: Males of this western species have sky-blue heads and upperparts, an orange-brown breast, and two white to buffy wing-bars. The females resemble rather nondescript sparrows, with unspotted tan breasts, dark brown upperparts, and two inconspicuous whitish buff wing-bars. Hybridization with the closely related Indigo Bunting (*Passerina cyanea*) occurs commonly in eastern Wyoming.

Voice: The male's song is a series of varied syllables, each repeated several times and often ending in a buzz. Males are tireless singers during the breeding season.

Status: A common summer resident, it winters in western Mexico.

Habitats and Ecology: The Lazuli Bunting inhabits shrub-dominated areas at varied foothills elevations, especially riparian vegetation and sagebrush. It forages among trees, shrubs, and on the ground, eating both seeds and insects.

JAN	FEB	MAR	APR	MAY	JUNE	JULY	AUG	SEPT	OCT	NOV	DEC
				xxxx	xxxx	xxxx	xxxx	xx			

Western Meadowlark (*Sturnella neglecta*)

Identification: Western Meadowlarks are one of the most abundant grassland songbirds in eastern Wyoming. Both sexes have bright yellow underparts and a conspicuous black V on the breast region. The upperparts are spotted and striped with
brown and buff, and the outer tail feathers are white, a field mark that is apparent
only during flight. Eastern Meadowlarks are extremely rare in Wyoming.

Voice: The male's song begins with a series of melodious whistles and descends to a series of gurgling warbles. Singing males often perch on wires or fence posts. A *chupp*
call is uttered by disturbed birds, and a harsh rattle is produced by fleeing birds.

Status: The Western Meadowlark is an abundant summer resident that winters in low
numbers along the lower North Platte River in southeastern Wyoming. Most birds
migrate to the southern United States and Mexico but local overwintering sometimes occurs, depending on weather conditions.

Habitats and Ecology: During the breeding season this species occupies open grasslands with thick litter layers of dead grass, including native mixed-grass prairies,
low-elevation mountain meadows, pastures, and hayfields (Faulkner, 2010). Early-
season haying during the nesting period is detrimental to this and many other
ground-nesting species.

JAN	FEB	MAR	APR	MAY	JUNE	JULY	AUG	SEPT	OCT	NOV	DEC
		xxx	xxxx	xxxx	xxxx	xxxx	xxxx	xxxx	xxx		

Gray-crowned Rosy-Finch (*Leucosticte tephrocotis*)

Identification: This small but seemingly fearless finch will fly directly into near-blinding snowstorms. It has a notched tail, a gray nape, a black forehead, and pink tints on its upper wings, belly, and rump. Its conical beak is yellow in winter, turning mostly black during the breeding season.

Voice: The winter call is a *chew* sound that can vary in frequency and number of notes. It seems to function as a contact call used when flocking.

Status: Common winter resident.

Habitats and Ecology: Birds that frequent this area in winter breed in the Rocky Mountains of northwestern Montana and possibly also in the Bighorn Mountains near Black Tooth Mountain, within the Cloud Peak Wilderness. They are extreme alpine breeders that descend in winter for food and shelter in response to severe winter weather. More than 1,500 birds have annually visited privately operated bird feeders located along Red Grade Road in the Bighorn Mountains foothills near Big Horn. Only a few flocks remain until April, when they leave for alpine breeding areas (V. Parham, personal conversation). Two regional subspecies are present: the brown-cheeked (*L. t. tephrocotis*) and the gray-cheeked Hepburn's (*L. t. littoralis*) races. The much rarer Hepburn's, shown here, composes only about 1 percent of Wyoming flocks (Faulkner, 2010).

JAN	FEB	MAR	APR	MAY	JUNE	JULY	AUG	SEPT	OCT	NOV	DEC
xxxx	xxxx	xxxx	xx						xxxx	xxxx	xxxx

House Finch (*Haemorhous mexicanus*)

Identification: In 1939, a few illegally captured birds from western North America were released from a pet store in New York City. The House Finches gradually spread west and within a half-century became one of the most numerous birds in the United States. Males have a red eyebrow and forehead, a brown cap, streaked brown flanks and underparts, and a slightly notched tail. Females and juveniles are streaked with brown overall and lack reddish markings. Males can be distinguished from the similar Cassin's Finch by their smaller beaks, slightly smaller bodies, and the absence of a red crown.

Voice: Males sing series of short warbling notes ending with an upward or downward slur. Singing sometimes occurs throughout the year, at least in warmer climates. Females sometimes utter a simpler version of the male's song.

Status: Abundant permanent resident.

Habitats and Ecology: This species is now generally associated with human habitations over most of its range, but it also uses undisturbed habitats such as grassland and riparian woodlands. Seeds, buds, flowers, leaves, and fruits are preferred foods. It feeds both on the ground and in trees and commonly visits bird feeders throughout the year.

JAN	FEB	MAR	APR	MAY	JUNE	JULY	AUG	SEPT	OCT	NOV	DEC
xxxx	xxxx	xxxx	xxxx	xxxx	xxxx	xxxx	xxxx	xxxx	xxxx	xxxx	xxxx

Cassin's Finch (*Haemorhous cassinii*)

Identification: This western finch resembles the House Finch but is chunkier, with longer wings and a longer heavier beak. The male has a well-defined bright red crown patch, with the back, breast, and flanks paler than in the similar House Finch. The streaks on the flanks and the malar stripe are also more apparent than the House Finch's. Females are a finely streaked olive-gray with distinctive brown ear patches.

Voice: The males' songs are series of short warbles, sometimes including imitations of the songs of other birds. Although their short vocalizations are species-specific, their longer songs often incorporate terminal syllables from other bird species. Calls are uttered by both sexes and consist of a series of *keeup* or *tidilip* notes (Hahn, 1996).

Status: A common permanent resident, the Cassin's Finch has altitudinal movements in spring and fall.

Habitats and Ecology: Common and conspicuous, this finch breeds in higher elevation coniferous forests of western interior mountains. Throughout the year it feeds on buds, berries, and seeds of conifers. In early fall the birds often forage with crossbills and other montane birds, and during winter they move southward and to lower elevations, often visiting bird feeders.

JAN	FEB	MAR	APR	MAY	JUNE	JULY	AUG	SEPT	OCT	NOV	DEC
xxxx	xxxx	xxxx	xxxx	xxxx	xxxx	xxxx	xxxx	xxxx	xxxx	xxxx	xxxx

Red Crossbill (*Loxia curvirostra*)

Identification: These birds occur throughout coniferous forests from Canada southward to the limits of spruce, pine, Douglas-fir, and western hemlock. Males are deep
brick-red to reddish yellow, with darker flight feathers. Females are olive to grayish, with a typical finch's notched tail and a yellowish breast and rump. All crossbills
have uniquely shaped mandibles that are strongly curved and crossed at their tips,
providing a prying tool that enables exposure and removal of seeds from closed
cones of various coniferous tree species.

Voice: Five populations that have distinctive call types, rather than being separate subspecies, have been identified in Wyoming. Birds of each call type tend to be associated with specific conifers and have associated foraging adaptations. Type 2 and
type 5 crossbills are specialized for extracting and feeding on ponderosa pine and
lodgepole pine seeds, respectively; both of these pines common in the Bighorn
Mountains region (C. W. Benkman, personal communication). Flight calls, often uttered by flocks, are *chip-chip-chip* . . . notes.

Status: A common permanent resident, the Red Crossbill varies locally in abundance
from year to year.

Habitats and Ecology: Breeding occurs in forests where there is an adequate food sup-
ply of coniferous cones. Variations in crossbill abundance result from their nomadic
movements in response to annual variations in seed availability (C. W. Benkman,
personal communication, December 13, 2016).

JAN	FEB	MAR	APR	MAY	JUNE	JULY	AUG	SEPT	OCT	NOV	DEC
xxxx	xxxx	xxxx	xxxx	xxxx	xxxx	xxxx	xxxx	xxxx	xxxx	xxxx	xxxx

Pine Siskin (*Spinus pinus*)

Identification: This rather small (5-inch) finch has a short, notched tail, a rather sharp but short beak, and a body that is mostly streaked with brownish and white but with yellow markings at the base of the tail and the inner flight feathers. Siskins are usually found in small groups and almost always are associated with conifers.

Voice: The Pine Siskin's song is a goldfinch-like series of trills, long down-slurring notes, and rolls and includes short ascending notes like those of the American Goldfinch but are lower and huskier. Their calls include a hoarse *teee* and a hoarse *jeeeah* note.

Status: Common permanent resident.

Habitats and Ecology: Breeding occurs in montane forests, especially high-elevation spruce-fir, cottonwood riparian, and aspen. Their foods are mainly conifer seeds but also include those of aspens. They seasonally feed on sunflowers and insects (Faulkner, 2010). The siskin population is unpredictably irruptive, with its abundance related to variations in seed crops during different years.

JAN	FEB	MAR	APR	MAY	JUNE	JULY	AUG	SEPT	OCT	NOV	DEC
xxxx	xxxx	xxxx	xxxx	xxxx	xxxx	xxxx	xxxx	xxxx	xxxx	xxxx	xxxx

American Goldfinch (*Spinus tristis*)

Identification: Breeding males have a bright lemon-yellow plumage except for a black forehead and notched tail, and mostly black wings except for white forewing patches. Females and winter-plumage males are much duller but have white (males) to pale buffy (females) wing-bars, a short and notched tail, a uniformly yellowish to brownish buff breast, and a short, stubby beak. The species' undulating flight and associated flight call are also diagnostic.

Voice: The social behavior of the American Goldfinch is associated with six distinctive vocalizations which include a *po-ta-to-chip* "contact call" uttered in flight, a "threat call," a *swee-ee* "alarm call," a *tee-yee* "courtship call," a high-frequency "feeding call," and a highly variable song (McGraw and Middleton, 2009). Male display flights in the breeding season are accompanied by song.

Status: Common permanent resident.

Habitats and Ecology: Breeding occurs in deciduous riparian areas, especially where thistles are abundant or cattails are found. The "down" of thistles or cattails is used in nest construction. Also, rather than insects, the seeds of thistles and other composite herbs are primarily used to feed the young. Deciduous riparian woodlands near weedy fields provide an ideal nesting situation. During winter the birds range widely over weedy fields and often visit bird feeders that provide thistle seeds or other tiny seeds.

JAN	FEB	MAR	APR	MAY	JUNE	JULY	AUG	SEPT	OCT	NOV	DEC
xxxx	xxxx	xxxx	xxxx	xxxx	xxxx	xxxx	xxxx	xxxx	xxxx	xxxx	xxxx

Checklist of Regularly Occurring Regional Birds

These 114 species include the abundant to uncommon birds of the region. Their taxonomy is in accordance with the 7th AOU *Checklist of North American Birds* as of 2016.

Regional abundance: A = Abundant, C = Common, U = Uncommon

Seasonal occurrence: PR = Permanent Resident, SR = Summer Resident,
M = Migrant, WM = Winter Migrant

Habitat: R = Riparian, W = Water, G=Grassland, M = Mountain Foothills, U = Urban

Species	Status	Habitat
Canada Goose	APR, WM	W
Wood Duck	USR	W
Gadwall	CSR	W
Mallard	APR	W
Blue-winged Teal	CSR	W
Green-winged Teal	CSR	W
Common Merganser	CPR	W
Gray Partridge	UPR	G
Ring-necked Pheasant	CPR	G
Sharp-tailed Grouse	UPR	G
Wild Turkey	CPR	R
Great Blue Heron	CPR	W
Turkey Vulture	CSR	G
Osprey	USR	R, W
Bald Eagle	USR, CWM	R, W
Northern Harrier	USR	G, W
Sharp-shinned Hawk	UPR	M, U
Cooper's Hawk	UPR	M, R
Northern Goshawk	UPR	M, U
Red-tailed Hawk	CSR, M	M, R, U
Rough-legged Hawk	CWM	G
Golden Eagle	UPR	G
Sandhill Crane	USR	R, W, G
Killdeer	ASR	G, W
Spotted Sandpiper	CSR	R
Wilson's Snipe	USR	W, R
Rock Pigeon	APR	U
Eurasian Collared-Dove	UPR	U
Mourning Dove	CSR	R, G, M, U
Eastern Screech-Owl	UPR	R, U
Great Horned Owl	CPR	R, U
Common Nighthawk	CSR	G

Checklist of Regularly Occurring Regional Birds

Species	Status	Habitat
_____ Calliope Hummingbird	CSR	R
_____ Broad-tailed Hummingbird	CSR	M, R
_____ Rufous Hummingbird	CM	M, U
_____ Belted Kingfisher	CPR	W, R
_____ Red-naped Sapsucker	CSR	M, R
_____ Downy Woodpecker	CPR	R
_____ Hairy Woodpecker	CPR	M, R
_____ Northern Flicker	CPR	R, U
_____ American Kestrel	CSR, WM	G, U
_____ Peregrine Falcon	USR	M
_____ Prairie Falcon	UPR	G
_____ Western Wood-Pewee	CSR	R, M, U
_____ Willow Flycatcher	CSR	R
_____ Least Flycatcher	CSR	R
_____ Say's Phoebe	CSR	G, U
_____ Western Kingbird	CSR	G
_____ Eastern Kingbird	CSR	G, R
_____ Loggerhead Shrike	USR	G
_____ Northern Shrike	UWM	M, G, U
_____ Warbling Vireo	CSR	R, U
_____ Red-eyed Vireo	CS	R
_____ Blue Jay	UPR	R, U
_____ Black-billed Magpie	CPR	G, U
_____ American Crow	CPR	G, M, U
_____ Common Raven	UPR	G, M, U
_____ Tree Swallow	CSR	R, W
_____ Northern Rough-winged Swallow	CSR	R, W
_____ Bank Swallow	USR	R, W
_____ Cliff Swallow	ASR	W, U
_____ Barn Swallow	CSR	W, U
_____ Black-capped Chickadee	CPR	R, M, U
_____ Mountain Chickadee	CPR	M, R, U
_____ Red-breasted Nuthatch	CPR	M, U
_____ White-breasted Nuthatch	CPR	R, U
_____ Brown Creeper	UPR	U
_____ House Wren	CSR	R, U
_____ American Dipper	CPR	W
_____ Ruby-crowned Kinglet	CSR	M, U
_____ Mountain Bluebird	CSR	G, M
_____ Swainson's Thrush	CSR	R
_____ American Robin	APR	M, R, U

Checklist of Regularly Occurring Regional Birds

Species	Status	Habitat
_____ Gray Catbird	CSR	R, M
_____ Brown Thrasher	USR	R, M, U
_____ European Starling	APR	U
_____ Bohemian Waxwing	CWM	R, U
_____ Cedar Waxwing	CPR	R, U
_____ Orange-crowned Warbler	CSR	R
_____ MacGillivray's Warbler	CSR	R
_____ Common Yellowthroat	CSR	R
_____ American Redstart	CSR	R
_____ Yellow Warbler	CSR	R, U
_____ Yellow-rumped Warbler	CSR	R, M
_____ Western Tanager	CSR	R
_____ Green-tailed Towhee	USR	M
_____ Spotted Towhee	CSR	R, M
_____ American Tree Sparrow	CWM	R, G, M, U
_____ Chipping Sparrow	CSR	R, N, U
_____ Brewer's Sparrow	CSR	G
_____ Vesper Sparrow	ASR	G
_____ Lark Sparrow	ASR	G, M
_____ Lark Bunting	ASR	G
_____ Savannah Sparrow	CSR	G, W, R
_____ Song Sparrow	CPR	R, W
_____ White-crowned Sparrow	CSR, UWM	M, G
_____ Dark-eyed Junco	CPR, CWM	M, G
_____ Black-headed Grosbeak	CSR	R, M
_____ Lazuli Bunting	CSR	R, M
_____ Bobolink	USR	G
_____ Red-winged Blackbird	CSR, CM	W
_____ Western Meadowlark	ASR	G
_____ Brewer's Blackbird	CSR	G, U
_____ Common Grackle	CSR	R, U
_____ Brown-headed Cowbird	CSR	G, U
_____ Bullock's Oriole	CSR	R, U
_____ Gray-crowned Rosy-Finch	CWR	M
_____ Pine Grosbeak	UR	U
_____ Cassin's Finch	CPR	U
_____ House Finch	APR	U
_____ Red Crossbill	CPR	U
_____ Pine Siskin	CPR	R, U
_____ American Goldfinch	CPR	R, G, U
_____ House Sparrow	CPR	U

References

The Birds of North America

The Birds of North America project is a multiauthor and joint publication effort begun in the early 1990s by the American Ornithologists' Union (AOU) and the Academy of Natural Sciences, Philadelphia, to monograph all the species of birds known to have bred within the boundaries of the United States and Canada. Individual species accounts have since become available online through the Cornell Laboratory of Ornithology, Ithaca, New York, on its website, https://birdsna.org. The following accounts are cited in this booklet.

Bartos, S. S., and J. S. Greenlaw. 2015. Spotted Towhee.

Bechard, M. J., and T. R. Swem. 2002. Rough-legged Hawk.

Bemis, C., and J. D. Rising. 1999. Western Wood-Pewee.

Boarman, W. I., and B. Heinrich. 1999. Common Raven.

Calder, W. A., and L. L. Calder. 1994. Calliope Hummingbird.

Connelly, J. W., M. W. Gratson, and K. P. Reese. 1998. Sharp-tailed Grouse.

Foote, J. R., D. J. Mennill, L. M. Ratcliffe, and S. M. Smith. 2010. Black-capped Chickadee.

Gerber, B. D., J. F. Dwyer, S. A. Nesbitt, R. C. Drewien, C. D. Littlefield, T. C. Tacha, and P. A. Vohs. 2014. Sandhill Crane.

Ghalambor, C. K., and T. E. Martin. 1999. Red-breasted Nuthatch.

Giudice, J. H., and J. T. Ratti. 2001. Ring-necked Pheasant.

Greenlaw, J. S. 1996. Spotted Towhee.

Hahn, T. P. 1996. Cassin's Finch.

Hudson, J. 1999. Western Tanager.

Hunt, P. D., and D. J. Flaspohler. 1998. Yellow-rumped Warbler.

Jackson, J. A., and H. R. Ouellet. 2002. Downy Woodpecker.

Johnson, L. S. 2014. House Wren.

Jones, S. L., and J. E. Cornely. 2002. Vesper Sparrow.

McCallum, D. A., R. Grundel, and D. L. Dahlsten. 1999. Mountain Chickadee.

McGraw, K. J., and A. L. Middleton. 2009. American Goldfinch.

Nolan, Jr., V., E. D. Ketterson, D. A. Cristol, C. M. Rogers, E. D. Clotfelter, R. C. Titus, S. J. Schoech, and E. Snajdr. 2002. Dark-eyed Junco.

Poole, A. F., R. O. Bierregaard, and M. S. Martell. 2002. Osprey.

Schukman, J. M., and B. O. Wolf. 1998. Say's Phoebe.

Trost, C. H. 1999. Black-billed Magpie.

Walters, E. L., E. H. Miller, and P. E. Lowther. 2014. Red-naped Sapsucker.

Wiebe, K. L., and W. S. Moore. 2008. Northern Flicker.

Witmer, M. C., D. J. Mountjoy, and L. Elliot. 2014. Cedar Waxwing.

Other References

Bent, A. C. 1942. *Life Histories of North American Flycatchers, Larks, Swallows, and Their Allies: Order Passeriformes*. Bulletin 179, Smithsonian Institution, Washington, DC.

Bent, A. C. 1946. *Life Histories of North American Jays, Crows, and Titmice: Order Passeriformes*. Bulletin 191, Smithsonian Institution, Washington, DC.

References

Brown, C., and M. Brown. 1988. A new form of reproductive parasitism in Cliff Swallows. *Nature* 331:66–68.

Canterbury, J., A. Downing, and P. Lecholat. 2016. *Bird Checklist for The Brinton Museum*. Big Horn, WY: The Brinton Museum.

Canterbury, J., and P. A. Johnsgard. 2016. *Bird Checklist of the Bighorn Mountains Region and Bighorn National Forest* (2-page species list).

Canterbury, J. L., P. A. Johnsgard, and H. F. Downing. 2013. *Birds and Birding in Wyoming's Bighorn Mountains Region*. Lincoln, NE: Zea Books. http://digitalcommons.unl.edu/zeabook/18

Ehrlich, P. R., Dobkin, D. S., and D. Wheye. 1988. *The Birder's Handbook: A Field Guide to the Natural History of North American Birds*. New York: Simon & Schuster.

Faulkner, D. W. 2010. *Birds of Wyoming*. Greenwood Village, CO: Roberts & Co.

Johnsgard, P. A. 1986. *Birds of the Rocky Mountains, with Particular Reference to National Parks in the Northern Rocky Mountain Region*. Boulder, CO: Colorado Associated University Press.

Johnsgard, P. A. 1988a. An analysis of migration schedules of non-passerine birds in Nebraska. *Nebraska Bird Review* 48:26–36.

Johnsgard, P. A. 1988b. An analysis of migration schedules of passerine birds in Nebraska. *Nebraska Bird Review* 48:46–57.

Johnsgard, P. A. 1997. *The Hummingbirds of North America*. 1997. 2nd ed. Washington, DC: Smithsonian Institution Press.

Johnsgard, P. A. 2002. *Grassland Grouse and Their Conservation*. Washington, DC: Smithsonian Institution Press.

Johnsgard, P. A. 2009. *Four Decades of Christmas Bird Counts in the Great Plains: Ornithological Evidence of a Changing Climate*. University of Nebraska–Lincoln DigitalCommons. 334 pp. http://digitalcommons.unl.edu/biosciornithology/46/

Johnsgard, P. A. 2015a. *A Chorus of Cranes: The Cranes of North America and the World*. Boulder, CO: University Press of Colorado. 242 pp.

Johnsgard, P. A. 2015b. *Global Warming and Population Responses among Great Plains Birds*. 2015. University of Nebraska–Lincoln and Zea Books. 384 pp. http://digitalcommons.unl.edu/zeabook/26

Johnsgard, P. A. 2016. *The North American Grouse: Biology and Behavior*. University of Nebraska–Lincoln and Zea Books. 183 pp. http://digitalcommons.unl.edu/zeabook/41/

Knight, D. H., G. P. Jones, W. A. Reiners, and W. H. Romme. 2014. *Mountains and Plains: The Ecology of Wyoming Landscapes*. 2nd ed. New Haven, CT: Yale University Press.

Meyer, C. B., D. H. Knight, G. C. Dillon, and K. Gregory. 2005. *Historic Range of Variability for Upland Vegetation in the Bighorn National Forest, Wyoming*. Denver, CO: US Department of Agriculture, Forest Service, Rocky Mountain Research Station.

Muir, J. 1894. *The Mountains of California*. New York: Century.

Reaume, T. 1988. Voice of the American Crow. *Ontario Birds* 6:23–24.

Rendall, D., and C. D. Kaluthota. 2013. Song organization and variability in Northern House Wrens (*Troglodytes aedon parkmanii*) in western Canada. *Auk* 130:617–628.

Scott, V. E., K. E. Evans, D. R. Patton, and C. P. Stone. 1977. *Cavity-Nesting Birds of North American Forests*. US Department of Agriculture, Agricultural Handbook No. 511.

Smith, S. M. 1991. *The Black-capped Chickadee: Behavioral Ecology and Natural History*. Ithaca, NY: Cornell University Press.

United States Congress. 1918. Migratory Bird Treaty Act (MBTA), U.S.C., 1918: 703–712.

www.ingramcontent.com/pod-product-compliance
Lightning Source LLC
Chambersburg PA
CBHW040130270326
41928CB00001B/19